WHAT BOOKS PRESS

AN IMPRINT OF

THE GLASS TABLE

COLLECTIVE

LOS ANGELES

ALSO BY MARIANO ZARO

DECODING
SPARROWS

MARIANO ZARO

LOS ANGELES

Publisher's Cataloging-In-Publication Data
Names: Zaro, Mariano, 1963- author.
Title: Decoding sparrows / Mariano Zaro.
Description: Los Angeles : What Books Press, [2019]
Identifiers: ISBN 9781532341458
Subjects: LCSH: Zaro, Mariano, 1963---Poetry. | Children--Spain--Poetry. | Coming of age--Poetry. | Spanish Americans--California--Poetry. | Intimacy (Psychology)--Poetry. | Desire--Poetry. | LCGFT: Poetry.
Classification: LCC PS3576.A73 D43 2019 | DDC 811/.54--dc23

Cover art: Gronk, *untitled*, watercolor and ink, 2018
Book design by Ash Good, www.ashgood.design

What Books Press
363 South Topanga Canyon Boulevard
Topanga, CA 90290

WHATBOOKSPRESS.COM

DECODING
SPARROWS

To A.M.S.

CONTENTS

THREE

ONE

PLUMS

My father wraps plums
with newspapers.
I cut the pages in half.
He wraps the plums.
We are in the attic.
It's summer.
We don't talk.

He rolls the fruit.
His fingers twist both ends of the paper.
It's raining outside.
The plums look like wrapped candy.

He is meticulous, not too meticulous, just enough.

The plums have to be without nicks or cuts,
firm, not too ripe, unblemished.

The storms have been coming all afternoon.
That's why my father is home;
he couldn't go to the fields.

He ties the plums with a thin string,
like a necklace.
Five plums in each string, exactly five.
I don't know why.
His hands inspect the fruit, twist the paper,
tie the knots, do the math.
I hide my hands under the newspapers.

He is on a ladder now.
He hangs the strings
from a wooden beam in the ceiling.
I pass the strings to him.
One by one.
Sometimes, unintentionally,
my hand brushes his hand.

He leans his body against the ladder,
rests for a moment,
cleans his sweat.
My father is old.

The strings dangle from the ceiling.
Plums in-waiting like dull,
modest Christmas ornaments.

Fruit for the winter, he says.
As if you could wrap the summer with newspapers.
As if you could wrap your father's hands
for the future days of hunger.

RED SWIMSUITS

We all wear red swimsuits
in this summer camp on the Mediterranean.
It's the rule, the uniform.
That way we are more visible
to the counselors taking care of us.
They are not really counselors,
they are still in college.

We swim at the beach.
It's so hot, the seagulls don't move.
Don't move on top of rocks,
on top of telephone poles.
We go back to the locker room,
we undress, we take a shower.
Today I cannot untie my swimsuit.
I have been in the water until the last minute.
The string is too wet, too tight.
I call one of the counselors.
He is tall.
All adults are tall when you are nine.
He tries the knot,
has big hands.
All adults have big hands.
It's too tight, he says.
He leans over
and unties the string with his teeth.
I feel his stubble against my belly,
for a second. Sandpaper, amber, mint,
danger at the border of flesh and fabric.
Go, hit the shower, he says.

I cannot move.
I lift my arms between crucifix and butterfly.
I lean against the lockers;
the metal doors rattle.
I see small, soft seagulls coming out of my chest.
Turquoise seagulls, aqua seagulls
that fly fast and hit the ceiling.
They scream, turn, open their beaks;
other seagulls come out of their mouths,
pink seagulls with red eyes.
Their wings on my throat,
on my eyelashes.

Finally, they find the narrow window,
they leave the room.

I am alone, the last one there.
From outside, somebody calls my name.
There is salt on the roof of my mouth.

WOMAN WITHOUT A NOSE

The first time I saw her,
it was at the doctor's office,
in the waiting room.

She was a woman
without a nose.
I was ten. She was old,
small, dark.
I was with my mother.
My mother took me many times
to the doctor's office,
but that's another story.

I know I was ten because
I had brought my math homework.
We were studying the binary system then,
we only did that in fourth grade.
One plus one was not two,
it was one-zero.
It was too complicated.
The school dropped it after a while,
and we went back to the routine of long division.

I was doing my math homework when she entered.
She came with her daughter, I believe.
The old woman did not have a nose.
She had the hole for the nose, not the nose itself.
A hole the shape of an inverted heart,
like a hazelnut.
A hole like the hole you see on a skull
where the nose used to be.

This skull was alive.
On top of the hole a tiny, white, pointy triangle—
the remains of cartilage.
I could not stop staring.

My mother tried everything,
Go, get me a magazine. Do your homework.
Don't you need to go to the bathroom?
I kept staring.

The woman said, *It's okay. He can look.*
Do you want to look? she asked me.
I went toward her. She was seated.

I stood in front of her, face to face.
I looked without restraint.
I wanted to see the inside of her head.
Does it hurt? I asked.
Sometimes, she said.

My mother apologized.
Don't worry, the woman said.

I saw her one more time, in church.
She had her nose covered
with a white gauze.
I said *hello*, she smiled back.

THE PAINTER

I take painting classes with him after school.
He is a starving artist.
My father gives him potatoes,
apricots, figs, peppers, artichokes.
They are friends, my father
the farmer and he, the painter.
That's why I don't pay for his classes.
It's called *bartering*.

He has other students in the studio, adults.
They pay. They look sophisticated to me.
They paint empty glass bottles,
broken pottery compositions;
things I never thought could be beautiful.
They paint portraits from photographs,
but I don't like them; they look deformed.

I am the youngest in the studio,
shy, lost in that cloud of turpentine,
in that spell of stained canvas.

I love the painter's hands. He can draw and paint
with both hands. *This is the hand of God,
this is the hand of the devil*, he says.
He sounds comical sometimes.
Sometimes I am afraid of him.

*No glass bottles, no pottery and
absolutely no portraits for you*, he says.
I cannot complain. I am not a paying student.

He tells me to close my eyes and draw what I see.
That's my first assignment.
It doesn't make sense. But I am obedient, I try.
I grab the pencil as you grab a pocket knife.
I draw circles with my eyes closed.

He is standing next to me.
I open my eyes, we look at my circles.
Good, he says. *Not a bad beginning.*

He opens one of the windows in the studio,
puts a chair next to it, tells me to sit and wait.

On the windowsill, he leaves
a tin box full of wax colors.
Not a small box like the one I have at school
with twelve colors. Twelve precise colors,
all organized, all labeled:
red, orange, light green.
This one has forty colors, fifty. I don't know.
The colors are used, all tumbled together,
sticky, contaminated.
They smell like dirty hands.

Now, take out the colors,
one by one. Take them out of the box,
put them on the windowsill.
But only the colors you see there.
Do you understand?
Only the colors you see there, he says.

instructions

10

And I look *there*. *There* is across
from the window. But I don't see
trees, *there*, mountains, *there*, a sunset.
I see the brick wall of the house
across the street. In the wall, a window
with an empty bird cage.
He leaves me alone.

The bricks are brown,
and I take out brown from the box.
The window is green,
and I take out green.
The cage is gray,
and I take out gray, and I am finished.

I have three colors on the windowsill
for a long time,
and I know this is not going well.
Then I look again, and I see a lonely
feather in the cage. There is some
red in the feather, some white,
and I thank God for that feather.
And I keep looking, and I see that
the bricks have black spots,
yellow spots. And I start
taking colors out of the box.
I take blue, because I see blue in the shadows,
because in desperation you see nothing
or you see everything.

I take colors out of the box,
one by one, almost all colors.
Until he comes back and without
saying anything he holds my head
with his hands; his fingers are warm.
I am between God and the devil.
He kisses my forehead.
I don't know if he is happy for me,
or sorry.
I feel his unkempt beard and mustache,
surprisingly soft.

use or change

The staircase is L-shaped
with a huge cactus in the corner.
Be careful with that,
my mother says every time
we go to visit my aunt Pepa.
Today we are there
because her son has died.

Her son was away, in college.
He wanted to be a lawyer but
liked music most of all.
He died suddenly, they say.

Everybody is in the kitchen,
my aunt and the neighbors,
all women, dressed in black.
My mother is not,
she didn't have time to change.

My aunt Pepa is sitting in a low chair,
she looks smaller than ever.
My mother and my aunt are cousins.
They hug, cry, don't really talk.
My mother grabs my arm,
brings me closer to my aunt.
I kiss her. She is cold, the air is cold.
A neighbor brings a couple of chairs.
He was so young, somebody says.
Nobody knows how he died.
We sit down.

The kitchen smells like bleach.
There is no food around.
I never have seen
the kitchen like this—
so clean, empty,
all pans and pots
put away in the cupboards,
no fruit in the fruit bowl,
no dish in the dish rack,
no bread.

I look at my mother.
Where is the body? I want to say.
My mother whispers in my ear.
He is in the hospital.
They have to do an autopsy.
Somehow my aunt hears us
and she breaks down
and sobs as if the word *autopsy*
is even worse than the word death.

I notice that the TV is covered
with a white tablecloth,
so is the large mirror over the credenza.
The mirror is a sailboat.
More neighbors come.

What's an autopsy? I ask my mother
as soon as we leave the house.
*They cut you open, they look inside
and then they sew you back together
with long stitches, as if they don't care,
as if they all were in a rush,* she says.
She stops and fixes the scarf
around my neck. *This wind,* she says.
What about the mirror? I ask.
Oh, the neighbors did that, she says.
It's because of the sadness.

NUN EATING A SMALL APPLE

We are on a bus,
my mother and I.
We are going to Zaragoza.
There is a nun sitting next to us.
She looks down,
hands crossed over a bag on her lap.
Fat fingers.

In the middle of the trip,
she takes out a small apple from the bag.
She offers the apple to me.
No words, just the gesture.
Thank you, my mother says.
I don't take the apple.

With her right thumb,
the nun makes the sign of the cross
over the apple's skin.
She starts eating.
The apple is crunchy.
The first bite is loud
and the nun covers her mouth with her hand.
She has a big piece of apple in her mouth.
She doesn't dare to chew it.
She cannot spit it out.
We look at each other.
She is probably embarrassed at her hunger.
The loud apple is her penitence.

After a while
she keeps eating
with small, silent, careful bites.
She keeps eating
until there is almost nothing left,
just the thin, bare core of the apple.
No seeds remain.
Wasting food would have added
another sin for confession.

When she is finished,
she hides the core of the apple in her hand,
presses her lips with her fist.
I notice the apple's stem sticking out
like a rebellious appendix.

BALDOMERA

When Baldomera performs her own death,
we children sing to her
Baldomera, Baldomera,
se te ve la faltriquera.
Baldomera, Baldomera,
we can see your underwear.

She opens the front doors of the house,
drags an old mattress on the floor,
puts it in the center
with two candles, one on each side.
She dresses in white,
wears a little wreath of paper flowers,
grabs a rosary,
lies on top of the mattress
and waits.

Her face is white.
She is not sick, my mother has told me,
that's just rice powder.

We can see your underwear,
we can see your underwear,
we sing.

We sing until she gets up
and runs and chases us
through the streets.
Sometimes she loses her wreath.
The paper petals fly away.

We are young, she is old.
We run faster, we escape.
One day, one day I will catch you all, she says.

And I know it doesn't matter
how fast I run, how young I am.
One day she will catch me,
like a dog that bites your ankle
and doesn't let go.

FIGS

I planted this fig tree the day you were born,
my father tells me.
The tree is tall, abundant, with dense shade.
It's my twin brother.

When in season, I bring figs to friends and neighbors.
Figs organized in concentric circles,
on a tray that my mother lines with fig leaves.
I also bring figs to my Uncle Santiago.
Don't knock at his front door,
go through the garage, my father says.
My mother doesn't put the figs on the tray,
she puts then inside a paper bag.
My uncle Santiago is diabetic.
You are killing him. He cannot eat figs, his wife says.
I deliver the figs through the garage.
He is waiting. *Thank you for the contraband*, he says.
He gives me a coin, kisses the top of my head.
He eats the figs right there, in the garage,
without turning the lights on.
He opens the figs' skin with his thumbnail.

My Uncle Santiago is not my uncle. We call him uncle
because he grew up with my father.
My grandmother breastfed both of them.
And somehow they look alike, my father and Santiago—
tall, soft grey eyes, quiet.

use of dialouge

Your fig tree is sick, my father says one summer.
He also says the word *fungus*.

The tree looks normal but when you turn the leaves
you can see little white spots, in clusters.
I go with my father to the pharmacy,
we buy some kind of powder, my father mixes it with water.
We cannot spray the tree now, it's too hot, my father says.
We have to wait until the sun goes down.

After we spray, the tree leaves start dripping—
a small, toxic rain that hits the ground. *Stay away,* my father says.
I ask, *Is the tree dying?*
Everything that breathes is dying, he says.

Could we plant another tree? I ask.
We could, but it takes a long time until it bears fruit.
Years. You will plant your trees one day, my father says.

My limbs feel heavy. I press my arms alongside my body.
I want to go home. Hide.
I don't want my father to wait in vain.

THREE DELIVERIES AND A ROOM
CALLED "SOL Y SOMBRA"

Her forehead leans against the only window in the kitchen.
She is crying. The apartment is attached to the police station.
She is *La Capitana*, the wife of the Captain.

Leave the groceries on the counter, her cook tells me.
I am the delivery boy. Today I brought strawberries,
asparagus, eggplants and one small watermelon.

Why is she crying? I whisper. *Nobody knows,* the cook says.
She will give you the tip next week. Don't bother her.
I understand, I say. *Goodbye Señora.* She doesn't respond.

It's summertime and I work at my aunt Teodora's store.
She doesn't pay much but the customers give decent tips.
You are so kind, they say. I am tired of being so kind.

Take these bags to Doña Sonsoles Álvarez, my aunt tells me.
I like going to her house. I like the garden, the fountain,
the tamarind trees, the marble steps. I wait in the hallway.

Maybe one day she will invite me to go inside where
people are never in a hurry and curtains float
alongside tall balconies. The maid takes the bags to the kitchen.

There is a coat hanger with silk scarves printed with stirrups,
saddles and bridles. I don't touch them.
I prefer to imagine how soft they are, how sweet they are.

Doña Sonsoles gives me the tip all at once, at the end of the summer.
Clean bills, as if ironed, in a small envelope
with a handwritten note. Powder blue stationery, simple signature.

I also have to help Ernestina Berrueco. *You have to help her
because she lives alone*, my aunt says. She lives alone
in a big mansion she inherited from her father.

Her father's name still on the enamel plaque at the front door:
Antonio Berrueco, Smelting Corporation.
Ernestina wears seersucker suits, white shirts.

Always in a suit. I wonder if those are her father's suits,
her father's shirts. Sometimes she smokes.
I have never seen her outside her house.

Leave the bags in the sol y sombra, she says.
The *sol y sombra* is a room in the middle of a long corridor.
The door is ajar, forty-five degrees.

Open enough for me to see, on the right, a formal office—
heavy desk, velvet chair, leather bound books, a floor lamp.
When you enter the room, on the left, the pantry.

In the pantry, metal shelves, rows of sealed glass jars with
whole peaches and pears; flour packages, cans of olive oil,
wood crates with onions and potatoes, dried peppers.

That's where she gives me the tip. In the *sol y sombra*,
on that confused line between the office and the pantry.
Don't spend it all, start saving, she says.

Thank you, Doña Ernestina, I say. *This is a small town*, she says.
Everybody knows everything. Have you thought about leaving?
I mean one day, when you grow up, in the future.

OLD PETRA

Old Petra lives alone at the end of the street
with a pet monkey named Ximo.
He is an inheritance.
Petra wears long black skirts.
Ximo is a well-dressed monkey.
She makes vests for him: forest green corduroy,
gray satin with pearl buttons, denim,
studded black leather.

Ximo was the mascot of a rock band.
Petra's son was the lead singer.

She still has a faded poster in the living room.
The Ximos—five men with long hair,
tight pants, a drum set and a monkey.
They had a bad car accident one night.
I think somebody died.
Ximo still remembers the accident.
That's what Petra says.
Some days he hides in a corner,
shivering, for no reason.

We children go to visit Old Petra,
just to play with the monkey.
We give him peanuts, sunflower seeds,
candy that he crushes with his pointy teeth.
Ximo rubs his ears, as if cleaning something
impossible to clean. He is almost deaf.
Too many concerts tied to the loudspeakers,
Petra tells us.

We give him apples cut in quarters.
We cover small pebbles
with candy wrapping, give them to him.
He drops them like dead birds.
Nobody can fool this monkey, Petra says.
He looks at us with human eyes,
without blinking.

Ximo often escapes
through the kitchen balcony.
Old Petra climbs to the roof.
Ximo, Ximo, she calls him.
The neighbors open the windows,
we gather around the house.

Come down Petra, we say, *come down*.
She walks on the roof like a frail marionette.
Come down crazy Petra, somebody says.

She gets mad, Old Petra. She reaches inside
her skirt pockets and throws clothespins,
old pieces of bread, wads of Kleenex
that don't reach the ground.

One day she threw a dirty fork
and then lifted her skirt,
opened her legs and peed on the roof.

Move away, my friends told me.
But I didn't move. I wanted to be close.

BABY DOLPHIN SUSPENDED
IN FORMALDEHYDE

You are coming with me
to Valencia, my sister says.
That's a long trip, my mother says,
all the way to the coast.
Five hours, my sister says.
It's better if I am away for a few days,
after what happened.

I am so happy to go to Valencia,
but I cannot say it.
I try to look serious, introspective,
as she does.

We go to Valencia because my sister
is not getting married
at the end of the month,
as was planned.
Because of some break-up drama,
some ultimatum.
Even the parents of the groom came
to talk to our parents.
There is nothing to talk about,
my sister said.

Her small car smells
like she smells: rose lipstick,
chamomile shampoo, hand cream.
We stop to get gas, coffee.

I clean the windshield splattered
with dead mosquitoes.
The hotel is near the beach, you know,
my sister says, *it has a swimming pool.*

It's raining when we arrive at the hotel.
Not the best day to go to the beach,
the receptionist says. *But you can go
to the Science Museum, it's walking distance.
They close at six. Children like it.*

The museum is an abandoned collection
behind glass cases.
Specimens with faded labels:
"Shark's Tooth," "Whale's Skull, Fragment,"
"Gorgonian Coral a.k.a. Sea Fan."

On a shelf, jars with dead animals
suspended in formaldehyde.
In one of them, a small dolphin—
face deformed, pressed against the glass,
eyes closed.
"Baby Dolphin. Valencia Harbor. 1963."
Look, I tell my sister, *1963, the year
I was born. A baby dolphin.*
Don't make me look at that, she says.
Not today.

There is a small shop at the exit.
A simple booth with keychains, magnets,
and a basket full of shells, starfish and seaglass.
I buy a shell the color of caramel.
My sister turns the shell over, runs her
finger along the edge—smooth, polished.
It's so beautiful, she says, *so intact*.
She is not wearing her ring.

We go back to the hotel,
running in the rain.
She covers her head with her purse.
Hurry up, she says.
I want to say something to make her laugh.
I have not seen her laughing
in a very long time.

Do you want a snack? she asks,
as soon as we are in the lobby.
At the empty snack bar
I order a sandwich, she orders coffee.
We sit at a low table facing the pool,
behind floor-to-ceiling windows.
The wicker chairs feel inappropriate
in this weather, out of season.
I like to watch the rain—
thin, consistent, over the pool's surface.

From one of the rooms on the first floor
a man walks toward the pool, undisturbed.
He wears a black swimsuit.
We look at him.
He has freckles, blond eyelashes,
strong shoulders.

My sister removes a strand of wet hair
from her forehead.
He must be a foreigner, she says.

The man jumps into the pool
and swims, to and fro, to and fro.
The rain becomes softer.

You should start shaving, my sister says.
And then she puts on her sunglasses
even though it's cloudy
and it's getting dark outside.
They are oversized sunglasses,
bright orange.
The man gets out of the pool,
walks back to his room.
The waiter brings the coffee.
Is everything okay, miss? he asks.
I don't dare look at my sister.

DOÑA MANOLITA,
THE SCHOOLTEACHER

With an atlas and a dictionary,
you can go anywhere, she tells me.

She is Doña Manolita, the Schoolteacher.
We all know that she is not a teacher.
She never finished her degree.

The two of us are in the bakery
where my mother works.
My mother has left me in charge today.

I like to be in the bakery, behind the counter,
with an apron that is too long for me,
the smell of sweet bread,
the smoothness of wrapping paper.

Wait for Doña Manolita, my mother says.
Tell her that the bread has been paid for.
You know what to do. Then, turn the lights off,
lock the door, and come home.

Doña Manolita is the last customer.
She comes on Tuesdays, late.

She always wears the same raincoat—
cream-colored, with a tight belt,
missing buttons and a muted shine on the collar.

The shine of over-brushed fabric.

What happened to Doña Manolita? I asked my mother once.
She was always peculiar, my mother told me.
But things became worse when she went to college.
She had strange thoughts. She was in an institution.

I also have strange thoughts.
I am afraid of the word *institution*.

Just two loaves of bread today, she says.
Doña Manolita caresses her raincoat lapels
as if caressing the last stitches of dignity.

I wrap two loaves of bread.
Here you are Doña Manolita, I say.
Crispy on the outside, as you like it.

How much is this, son? she asks.
You already paid for it last week, I say.
Don't you remember?

She looks at me. She has unusually long eyelashes,
pointing downwards,
lids heavy with eyeshadow.
Oh, that's right, she says. *I am losing my mind.*

Before she goes, she stops at the door.
See you next week, she says.

She lifts the bread up in the air, like a trophy.
Her raincoat opens, from belt down,
and reveals her satin slip, frayed at the edge,
stained in the center, baby blue.

DEAD NUN

Come with me to the convent, my mother says.
Sister Virtudes has died. Put on the wool hat,
and don't forget your gloves. It's freezing.

My mother and Sister Virtudes were friends.
Even though she could only leave the cloister
to go to the dentist, or to see a doctor.

We visited Sister Virtudes, used to take her
small tins of hand cream, unscented.
I know this is against the rules, my mother apologized.

The open coffin is not under the central dome.
It's in a small chapel, behind a tall wrought iron gate.
She doesn't look dead, my mother says. *Come closer.*

She doesn't look like Sister Virtudes, I tell my mother.
That happens to all dead people once the soul leaves
the body, my mother says. *But she looks beautiful.*

Sister Virtudes has fresh flowers across her forehead,
like a bride or a girl about to receive her first communion.
Those flowers, in the middle of winter, my mother whispers.

The nuns are around the coffin, all standing,
except an old nun sitting in a wheelchair,
her legs covered with a thick blanket.

Libera me, Domine, de morte aeterna, the nuns sing.
Libera me, Domine, de morte aeterna, we repeat.
I remove one glove, touch the hinge of the iron gates.

Mother, I say, *the nuns are not wearing socks.*
That's because of the mortification of the flesh,
she tells me. *What's mortification?* I ask.

The nuns stop singing. Silence floods the chapel.
A silence full of incense and the souls of all the nuns
who have died in the convent before.

It's time to go, my mother says. I want to leave
and I want to stay. The silence in me will be split open
one day, like a fruit that stains your hands.

We pass the sculpture of Gabriel, the Archangel,
fighting a naked Lucifer. Above the altar, the dove
of the Holy Spirit suspended on a silver cloud.

DECODING SPARROWS

My father and I on the balcony
watch dozens of sparrows walking
on the roofs across from us.
A sparrow doesn't really know how to make a nest, he says.
They are messy. Now, a stork, that's different.
A stork makes a perfect nest.

My father looks at the clouds.
Can you tell a male from a female sparrow? he asks.

No, I can't, I say.
What do they teach you in school, son? he says.
Look, male sparrows have a dark stain on the chest,
like a bib or an apron. Females don't.

And I look,
and there they are:
chests with aprons, chests without aprons.
Everything in order.
Dirty or clean,
white or black,
male or female.

I cross my arms against my chest.
My father doesn't look at me.
And then he says,
But we are not sparrows, you know.

TWO

THE ACTOR

Once in a while, he comes to see me in the dorm.
He comes unannounced. He sits on top of my desk
with his back against the window.
Can I smoke? he asks. I sit on the bed.
It's a small bed, not comfortable.
I had to put a wood plank under the mattress;
it was too soft. I couldn't sleep.
I still cannot sleep, but it's not because of the mattress.

In the room, there is a humble sink, a small mirror,
a glass shelf attached to the wall with rusty brackets.
On the shelf: toothpaste, shaving cream,
nail clippers. There is also a small plant,
a succulent that my sister gave me the day I left home.
This plant is indestructible, she told me.
But I know that it will die with me in this room,
like many other things.

I have dropped all my classes, he says.
I want to be an actor.
The sun hits his hair, and the hair is wheat,
flames, summer.
He opens the window, lights a cigarette,
keeps the hand outside.

I am going to the Avignon Theater Festival.
Would you like to come? he asks.
I don't know what to say. Avignon is far away.
I have no money. Avignon is for other people.

He turns toward the window,
looks at his reflection in the glass
and messes up his hair.
His profile is less impeccable now, less insulting.

It's getting dark. Under his thin cotton sweater,
his bony shoulders become harder, menacing.
There is no beauty without danger, they say.

He crosses his legs, knees almost touching
the Latin dictionary, my class notes,
and my journal where his name appears
in the same sentence, woven with other words—
grass, impossible, blond, balsamic, *azul* and magnolia.

PRIMO, THE JEWELER

He unrolls a cylinder of black velvet.
He says the names, and the stones appear—
amethyst, tourmaline, peridot,
citrine, garnet, obsidian.

With long tweezers he takes the stones
and places them, one at a time, on top
of my left ring finger. Not literally
on my finger, suspended just
above the skin.

How do you like this one? he asks.
He opens inkwells and tin boxes
with watercolors. He starts drawing.
He doesn't talk. Bent over the paper
he becomes small, absent.

He paints with tiny brushes and
sometimes with the tip of his fingers.
His fingers, soft and precise, know
my name, the arch of my ribcage,
the platform of shoulder blades.

He blows on the paper.
I can smell him—hair,
hands, the collar of his shirt.
The smell of him when we lived together,
the smell of breakfast on the kitchen table,
sitting next to each other
before the shower.

He gives me the drawing.
This is the way it's going to be, he says.
The piece feels heavy on the paper,
is still wet, has volume.
Now he talks and builds a house around me.
A house made of facets, inclusions,
karats, transparency, luster.

I feel protected and naked at the same time.
It's not easy to tolerate this proximity, this attention.

He looks old, for the first time.
He has been always the youngest of all,
the most precocious. *Primo,* I say,
you must be tired. He doesn't answer.

He must be tired of carrying
these stones every day,
from place to place—Brazil, Colombia,
India, The Netherlands. All his life
carrying these stones, keeping them clean,
intact, without a scratch, alive,
ready to craft antidotes for all of us.

SIRENO (MERBOY)

We study with the windows open
and the doors open.
There is no air conditioning.
Final exams are here.
It's the last week of June.

Few of us know his real name;
we call him Sireno,
and he is okay with it.
That's what we think.
Sometimes he even jokes about it.
I am a fishman, a fishman,
he shouts.

We study together tonight
in his room.
He wants to be a veterinarian.
He draws horses' heads in his notebooks,
sea urchins, sting rays, coral formations.
Where is the rain? he says.
Where is the rain?

He wears shorts, no T-shirt,
and carries a big, wet towel over his shoulders.
That's the way he studies every night
since the heat started.
The towel drips over the table;
his class notes get wet
and when the papers dry out
they are all curled, uneven.

We are sitting across from each other.
He has almost no hair,
no eyebrows, no eyelashes,
protruding eyes, flaky cheeks and temples.
He is beyond pale, has a pointy head.
Yes, he looks like a fish.

He has to use the wet towel because of his skin condition.
Ichthyosis, he told me when we met
in the beginning of the school year.
Tonight he tells me more about it.
This comes from my father's side.
My grandpa had the same thing, he says.

We all carry some kind of defective heritage.
Damages; some visible, some invisible.
Crippled messages segmented
in each cell's nucleus. We pass them on.
We cannot contain them between our legs.

Because of the heat his skin gets too dry,
brittle to the verge of bleeding.
Tonight he gets up often
to wet the towel in the sink.
We can hear the other students in the dorms.
Some of them are sitting at the windowsills,
smoking, talking into the night.

Sireno gets up one more time,
closes the door,
removes his shorts,
puts some lotion on his legs, his arms.
His underwear is white, small, provincial.
The lotion is medicated,
smells like disinfectant.

Could you do my back?
He never has asked before.
He stretches his arms,
turns, leans against the wall
with the palms of his hands wide open.
Like a detainee, like a prisoner.
I know it's disgusting, he says.
You can use a small towel if you want,
you don't have to touch me.

I don't use the towel,
I touch his skin.
His back is bumpy, rough,
like a warm reptile.
I do his back. I do his legs,
the inner part of his legs,
softer, but very scaly.

There is something repulsive about it,
something that clogs the back of my throat,
but I keep rubbing his skin
as if I deserve the repulsion.

I wish I could do something for you, he says.
You already have, I say.
He breathes heavily now,
drops his arms,
walks away from the wall,
goes to the sink,
wets his towel again.
There he is, standing in his white underwear,
a wet towel in his hand.

Do you think I will find somebody one day? he asks.
Sure, I say.
Well, I don't see many mermaids around, he says.

He starts dancing around the room,
or swimming. We start laughing.
For a moment, we almost forget the heat.

THE ACTRESS

María Elena eats a yogurt a day,
low fat, not at once. And little more.
Some baby carrots, perhaps,
a rice cake.
Eating makes me dirty.
But people don't know
that I am always hungry.
This is what she told me once,
between rehearsals.

We are in the same theater class.
We rehearse in the evenings
and all-day Saturdays
in a warehouse
that used to be a furniture store.

She comes late, María Elena.
She still has one third of the yogurt,
intact, in the container.
She closes the lid with Scotch tape
so she can carry the yogurt in her purse.
She also carries a white plastic spoon
and her baby carrots.
Because of all the carrots she eats
the skin of her hands is turning orange,
pale orange, not the whole skin,
that line where the palm becomes
the back of your hand,
that perimeter.

Sometimes María Elena sucks the empty spoon,
when she is distracted, looking away.
She has sunken cheeks,
that thing that looks so good in the movies.

She is Neighbor #1 in a play by Lorca,
the pregnant neighbor.
She refuses to wear the small,
round pillow under her dress.
I think the director has given up on that.

She also has a short monologue,
and at the end,
you can hear the effort
of her breathing, when she inhales,
you can see the veins on her neck,
the pasty white saliva,
the thick hairs on her arms
against the light,
the ribs through the fabric.
She has no breasts.

When she is finished
she puts on her coat,
tightens the belt
around her waist,
looks inside her purse,
lies down on an old couch,
and falls asleep.

I wake her up
when the rehearsal is over—
her arm on her face,
at an angle.
On the floor,
the plastic spoon
covered with teeth marks.

THE PHILOSOPHER

When we go to his apartment
there is a girl sleeping at the door,
curled up like a dog.
Not tonight, sweetie, he tells her,
I have company.

She leaves without a word.
I am the company.

We met long ago
at a birthday party.
He was my friend Clara's boyfriend,
he was also an assistant professor,
the youngest,
in the Philosophy department.
They made a great couple together,
he and Clara.
They were beautiful
without trying,
beautiful when tired, when dirty,
under the wrong light.

Too many girls, my friend told me
when they broke up.

Today we run into each other
in a bar where he used to go
with Clara. And we talk.
He talks in that voice that

tells you *Hey, you are the only one here.*
A voice made of walnuts
and secrecy and surrender.

We play the syllogism game,
the one we played with Clara,
always starting with
Socrates is a man,
all men are mortal,
therefore, Socrates is mortal.
He wants to try something else, he says.
Some stones become birds,
a canary is a bird,
therefore, some canaries are stones.

You just tell me where
you want me to stop.
This is the first thing I say
when we are both
inside the apartment.

He takes me to the window.
Look, he says.
You see these balconies?
The window faces an inner patio.
People enclose the balconies,
with glass panels.

They gain, how much?
Five more square feet
for the living room,
for one more chair.
They work hard for one more chair.

I kiss him because that's
what I have to do, what I want to do.
And I look at him and he looks
at his reaction and he undresses—
no underwear.
I notice that his apartment
is really dirty, with worn-out furniture,
that the curtain rail hangs uneven
like a broken arm.

His sex is dark, darker
than the rest of his body,
foreign against the pale
frame of the hips.
It's also luminous and crisp
like an unopened morning.

Your chest is hard,
it's full of ribs, he says,
when we are in bed.
And then he faces down,

all stretched like a board.
Turn a little, it's easier
if you are on your side, I say.
He turns, but the body is too tight,
and I become a useless locksmith
of fingertips and saliva.

Socrates is a man,
all men are mortal, I say.
He says, *Therefore Socrates is mortal.*
And there, when he says *Socrates,*
in that last "s" his body opens
and I go in without pushing
or moving, nothing.

I rest my forehead on his neck,
the back of his neck.
Son of a bitch, he says.
We run, we think we run,
without touching the floor.
We run in a dense forest
with tall, violent ferns,
ferns as tall as we are,
tall as fighting bears
or horses.
We are hit by branches,

pine needles, brambles,
we have lacerations,
apertures for air and mud
in the flesh,
for one more forest.

The next day the light wakes me up
but he is not there. He is sitting
in the kitchen, naked, with his legs up on a chair.
The ankles crossed,
the sex smooshed between the thighs,
skin tense, with thin violet veins,
more a tumor than a fruit.

I made some coffee, he says,
but there is nothing to eat,
some ice cream, maybe.
I want to say, *Let me go out*
to get some pastries, but I don't.
He is reading something,
correcting papers.
I drink my coffee.
He turns a page.

THE NEIGHBOR

He snores, I look at him.
He wakes up.
I did not cry as much today, he says.
The dogs bark outside, a plane goes by.
We want to believe that everything is as usual.
There is a painting on the bedroom wall—
a small bird carrying a box, a big box.
It has always been there, since I met him.
Today the box looks too heavy.

He eats the cheese and the crackers
against the doctor's orders.
I am not looking.
Then he needs to go to the bathroom.
He is too frail.
He doesn't make it.
I clean him.
You always wanted a piece of my ass,
he says.
The humor is still there,
it makes the awkward more manageable.

I open the window, wash my hands, take out the trash.
Come back. Wash my hands again.
I feel guilty when I wash my hands the third time.
And then he asks me questions.
I close the window to gain some time.
I don't know what to say.
I don't know what helps him more—

what I tell him, what I hide.
Maybe nothing can help at this stage.

He falls asleep again,
snores louder than we could expect
from a body like that.

THE CARETAKER

In a few weeks, my father will die
from prostate cancer in the University Hospital
of Zaragoza. He is seventy-five.

Many nights I stay with him in the hospital.
My shift is from eight p.m. to eight a.m.,
until my sister comes to replace me.

One Friday my sister comes earlier,
around six thirty in the morning.
I cannot sleep, she says. We are a family of bad sleepers.
Before going to my apartment, I stop in a café.
They are just opening. I sit at the counter.

There is a young man next to me. He is going home
after a night out with his friends.
That's what he tells me, and I believe him.
He looks calm, shy, sober, almost embarrassed.

I don't tell him about my father.
I don't want pity.

We don't need much negotiation.
I finish my croissant, he finishes his coffee.
We go to his apartment.
It's around the block.
I just moved in, he says.

There are unopened boxes and piles of clothing
on the floor, but the place feels organized,

welcoming. It's a one-bedroom apartment but
still, he shows me around.

Anything to drink? he asks. Inside the fridge
I see glass containers with food. *My mother
has given me this*, he says. *Are you hungry?*

He takes a shower, leaves the door open
and talks to me. *Do you want to take a shower?
Sit wherever you can. It will take me a minute.*

He comes to bed with his hair still wet.
He is thin, has long legs, small waist.

He has a tan line. I touch it
with the tip of my fingers.
Childhood is not too far away.
The days at the pool, the thirst,
the first time naked in front of other boys.

I don't sleep much.

When we wake up, I take a shower.
He gives me an orange towel.
The towel is inside a transparent
plastic bag. The day is almost over.
I have to go home and change
and go back to the hospital.

He writes his number on a piece of paper
but I never call.

TAXI DRIVER

He tells me that his wife is pregnant,
he just learned about it.

He is the taxi driver,
I am the passenger.

This happens at five in the morning,
in a taxi, on my way to the Madrid airport.

The taxi driver is young, handsome,
probably as handsome as he will ever be.
He is going home after this ride, he says.
He cannot wait.

Everything has a higher purpose now,
I suppose:
the way he stops at traffic lights,
the way he rolls up the window.

He drives through the city—
Cibeles, Recoletos, Castellana—
and the city turns and collects cells, tissue,
cartilage, bones, lungs for this child.
Madrid is the big spinning wheel
of embryos and invagination.

It happened so fast, he says.
We didn't know it was going to be so fast.

I want to ask him if he knew
exactly when the conception happened.
If he felt anything different,
a stronger pulse, almost painful,
in that region between anus and
scrotum, in that equinox of flesh.

I don't ask anything,
I don't think it's appropriate.
So I say the things you say on these occasions:
Congratulations, all the best to you and your wife.
I watch him driving his smooth drive,
the one I will never drive.

When we arrive to the airport,
he helps me with my luggage and I thank him.
I pay, give him a tip. Suddenly he hugs me.
Have a good trip, he says.

I can't tell if he knows what I am thinking,
what I want from him.

THE MUSICIAN

I fold your shirts.
We are going to San Sebastian.
We are in Madrid, in your parents' house.
Your parents are off for the week.
We are almost finished packing.
You are not sure about your shoes.
You can always buy shoes there, I say.
This is long ago. We are in our early twenties.
No, we won't have time; you know how it is, you say.
I open your closet, fold a sweater;
nights can be cold in the North.

We had sex the night before in your parents' bed.
I slept on your father's side.
I saw his reading glasses on the night table.
He forgot his reading glasses, I said.
You said, *Don't worry, he has glasses everywhere.*

Let me go to the shoe store,
down the street, just a moment, you say.
I am alone now in your parents' house.
I never have been alone here before.
I steal a small picture of you, not framed,
a loose leaf leaning against the books in a bookshelf.
A picture of you playing piano, even thinner, adolescent.
The picture is taken from the back,
but it's you—the shape of the head, the neck angle,
your right hand suspended, unmistakable.

Both suitcases wait on top of the bed.

You come back from the shoe store.
How do you like my new shoes? you say.
They are light, made of leather and canvas,
with double stitching on the sides.
Somehow you look younger.
You don't notice that I have taken the picture.
I am surprised. You notice everything.

We go to San Sebastian, you drive.
We stop a couple of times to pee.
We arrive, check into the hotel,
meet your friends in a bar.

We walk the streets, up and down, we get drunk.
You talk about music, as usual.
You tell me everything about Tchaikovsky's death,
and the affair he had with his nephew Vladimir,
also known as Bob.

And then you sing, you tell me to sing with you.
I cannot sing, I am tone deaf, but I sing anyway,
at the top of my lungs,
in a parking lot near the beach.
You cannot stop laughing.
I never have heard anything like that, you say.

The early morning buses are already running.
People go to work, have things to do.

Back in the hotel room you take off your shoes.
They hurt, you say.
We go right to bed.
The sunlight bothers you. I get up, close the curtains.
Outside the window,
two birds perch on the iron railing.
They have big heads, disproportionate.
One of them hits the glass with its beak.
Look, I say, *Tchaikovsky and his nephew Vladimir.*
You are already sleeping, on top of the bed,
face down, in your underwear.
You have blisters on your ankles.
I want to rub my hair against them,
I want to hold your feet
and say something tender.
I am too embarrassed.
Sometimes we mistake love for embarrassment.

I never told you about the stolen photograph.
Some secrets need to stay alive.
I never told you about the birds in the window.

I am afraid if I tell you
the birds will fly away,
we will disappear.

MASTER OF UNEVEN LINES

You print rolls of wall paper
with large rubber stamps.
It's my first time in this studio
you are renting outside London.
Your hair is long now.
You had short hair when we met.
My friends said you looked like Montgomery Clift.

The studio has a small kitchen
and a big armoire full of paint cans,
chisels and cardboard cutouts.
Do you sleep here? I ask.
On top of the armoire, you say.
I say, *Isn't it toxic? With all this paint, I mean.*
Oh no, you say, *it's just water,*
ground minerals and clay.

There are dirty dishes in the sink,
paint brushes, coffee mugs.

Some people pay a lot money for this paper, you say.
All handmade, one of a kind.

You spread the rolls over a long table.
We start talking.
You press the rubber stamps.
Red paint over light brown paper.

You need four stamps for each section, you see.
To complete the design.
You always knew how to explain everything.
And for a while, I was too willing to understand.
This is for a library in a Victorian house, you say.

You lift the stamps, carefully.
The paint glistens,
the symmetry appears—red birds standing
on red branches with red leaves and red berries.
The figures connect—bird against bird,
branch against branch. Leaves and berries
scattered and yet, organized.
The lines are uneven.
You are a master of uneven lines.

I feel dizzy all of a sudden, for no reason.
Sit down, you say, *here.*
And I sit on a bench, near the window.
Maybe the paint is toxic after all,
maybe it's low blood pressure.

You go to the sink and bring me
a glass of hot water. You take a sip
to make sure it's not too hot.
Drink, you say.
I drink, close my eyes.
Your color is coming back, you say.
My ears stop ringing.

You kneel down, grab my legs with your arms.
Your breath is dense, persistent, almost wet
when you rest your head on my lap.

LA POETA AND HER HUSBAND
AT THE MERIDIAN HOTEL

She eats a sardine. Vertically.
Not a sardine, a small herring
marinated in olive oil, vinegar and garlic.
She pinches the herring by the tail,
lifts it from the plate, calculates the timing
of the dripping oil, tilts her head back,
opens her mouth and eats the herring
in a single mouthful.
She blots her lips with a thin paper napkin.
Her pink blouse still immaculate.

She is sitting on a stool
at the bar in the lobby of the Meridian Hotel.
Her husband looks at her.
He is always looking at her with his mouth open.

We met in this bar, when the hotel opened,
he tells me. *When this was the best place in town.*
She was not even eighteen.
He asks me, *What are you studying?*
Literature, I say.
Don't you want to be a dermatologist?
They make a lot of money, he says.
He has trouble with the word dermatologist,
he has to repeat it several times until he gets it right.

They are both dressed up.
She wears a velvet skirt, rhinestone earrings,
and a sequined clutch the shape of a butterfly.
He wears a tweed suit, a paisley tie.
The gold-leaf of the tie pin, peeling off.

We don't know their names.
We call them La Poeta and El Poeta.
She is a poet. I don't think he writes anything.
I have an offering, she says sometimes.
We all gather around her to listen to her poems.
Her face gets sweaty when she reads, her cheeks flush.

All the rooms in the Meridian are closed off,
the windows boarded up. Only the lobby is open.
Students with no money go to the bar.
We drink cheap wine under tarnished sconces
and heavy chandeliers with dead lightbulbs.

You know, we couldn't have children,
she tells me. *I thought he was going to leave me*
when we learned about it. But he didn't.

They dance some nights, belly against belly,
their small, happy hands together.
They dance oblivious to the music,
oblivious to the scratched marble floors
covered with peanut shells.
That's why we go to the Meridian,
because nobody cares how you dance,
because the peanuts are free.

You look tired today, she tells me.
She opens her clutch and gives me
a piece of chocolate wrapped in foil.
Eat it, she says. *This is what I eat when I am down.*
The chocolate is muddy, granular, bitter.
You will feel better one day, she says.
You will find what you are looking for.

KITCHEN ORACLE

We are both in your kitchen,
in your parents' kitchen,
in the house they have outside Madrid,
where you spent your summers as a child,
where you now spend your weekends.

We will spend our weekends here, you tell me.
You are cooking dinner,
it's the end of May.
You are frying sardines.

It's very convenient, this house.
It's in the countryside
but not too far away from the city, you say.

You turn and show me the fish in the frying pan.
Fish with heads and tails and eyes.
I am setting the table.
Could you open the window? I ask.
Every single window is open, you tell me.

Look, just the way you like your fish,
with the skin almost burnt, you say.
Sometimes kindness feels like a long,
thin, silver needle.

It's fine, I say.
We know it's not fine.
Has not been fine for a while.
You turn off the stove.

I cannot stand the symmetry of the table:
two plates, two forks,
love, pity,
two glasses, two knives.

PORTRAIT AND STILL LIFE WITH ART

I worked in a hardware store, she tells me.

We are in Granada, in a hotel in Granada.
It's early in the morning. We are having breakfast.
She holds the coffee cup with both hands.

You have beautiful hands, I tell her.
They are okay for an old woman, she says.

I worked in a hardware store, in Brooklyn,
with an Italian girl, she says.
One day her brother came to the store.
The Italian boy.

I was selling nails, hammers, plaster.
I think I was in love with the Italian boy.
I was selling rivets, washers, spackle.
I was seventeen.

Nothing really happened.
We went to a dance once.
I thought it was dangerous to go to a dance with him.
Maybe it was shame.
They say shame is premature exposure.
They say shame is the seed of self-destruction.
I remember exactly what I was wearing—
a red, quilted skirt, a blouse with see-through sleeves,
and the black and white shoes.
I looked like a fool.

Other guests come down for breakfast,
foreigners, Germans, I think.

He made me nervous, the Italian boy.
I didn't know what to do with it.
Where to put it.
I could not contain it.
I didn't even have a container.

She orders another *café con leche.*
I like the way she says *café con leche.*
She sounds like a girl.
I tell her.

I hope I don't sound sweet, she says.
I don't like sweet, all these sweet people,
all these sweet girls; they know how to do sweet.
I don't trust sweet.

He is probably dead now, the Italian boy, she says.
He is probably dead in a Brooklyn cemetery.

I married the engineer, instead.
My parents liked him.

She eats a piece of toast.

I got married because I didn't know how to say no.
You spend your life trying not to hurt people.

We got married; it was the thing to do.
Very early I knew I had made a mistake.

I wanted to talk to people about it
but everybody was busy.
They tell you that is normal, that you feel strange
when you get married, in the beginning.
We were all busy trying to survive.

This happened when everything was there for me to have.

I don't blame anybody.
I don't want to make it nice.
I don't like sweet; I already have told you.

She stops talking, looks at the toast.

She picks up tiny crumbs,
presses the tablecloth with the tip of her ring finger.

THE CARD PLAYER

I go with my mother to the nursing home
to visit some of her friends.

She wears her navy-blue suit,
sand-colored blouse, and a pearl necklace.
The pearls are large and irregular,
deep gray on the verge of purple.
For a woman of ninety,
the necklace is almost too daring.

It's late June, the afternoon is warm,
everybody sits at two big tables near the garden.
The women sit together, the men sit together.
That's the way it is. The French doors are open
but nobody sits outside. *Too much of a risk,* they say,
you can never trust the weather.

My mother sits at the women's table.
They all talk at the same time.
Somebody mentions my mother's necklace.
They ask questions. They don't wait for answers.
They list illnesses, symptoms,
names of people who died recently.
They do the math; the years since the husbands died.
Almost twenty years, my mother says.

At one point the table gets quiet;
some women fall asleep,
or they just close their eyes.

My mother walks to the men's table.
They are playing cards. They don't talk much.
One of them turns his chair and places his cards,
face down, on top of the green felt.
He is not facing the table now, he is facing my mother.
Then, he says, *That's a nice necklace you are wearing.*
At the same time, he opens his legs.

There is nothing strange about it.
A man sitting on a chair opens his legs.
But my mother covers her necklace with her left hand.
She talks to the other men.
They stop the game for a moment.
She doesn't sit with them. She says goodbye.
She keeps her hand on top of the necklace
until we leave the room.

THREE

TALK IN MALIBU

+ dialouge

I pay in cash at the front desk.
The room is under your name.
I pay in cash before we go upstairs.
I don't want to be bothered the next day
with the transaction.
I don't want anybody to know that I am here.
I pay in cash, almost 200 dollars.
The room is in Malibu,
in a hotel in Malibu.

I lie to everybody today.
I tell my friends in the North
that I am in the South.
I tell my friends in the South
that I don't know where I will be this evening.

I don't lie to you.
I tell you that I will pick you up at four o'clock.
And there I am, at four, and there you are—
with no luggage, only a small brown paper bag
and a sweater. You wait with a paper bag
and a sweater. I will lie to you later.

We go to Malibu,
to a hotel room in Malibu—
ocean front,
with a ceiling fan.

In the corridors, we see a family
with small children. The mother is young,
looks friendly. I smile but don't say anything,
don't want to be seen, don't want the kids
to know what we are doing.

The room is white, not new,
old enough to feel real.
It has vines outside.
We open the window,
we don't need the ceiling fan.
The ocean is loud and close.
It doesn't pay attention to us.
We lie on the bed and talk.

We talk to say all we could not say before.
For months we have seen each other,
but we couldn't talk.

Now we talk. We probably have sex in between.
We don't stop talking. I get up to go to the bathroom.
I come back to bed. We whisper.
We press against each other. Sometimes we cry.
You can cry and talk at the same time.
You are very good at it.

We keep talking.
We talk our life together.

You imagine what you would tell me
when I leave for a long trip,
when I come back, when I wake up cranky,
when I am sick, when you have doubts, when I lose my hair.
I imagine what I would tell you
when we come home after your father's funeral.

We talk our life together, the life that won't happen.

We don't know how to end the talking,
we don't know how to end the craving.

We want the ocean to revolt
and come through the window and take us.

Take us and finish this talk for us,
so we don't have to decide, we don't have
to hurt each other now that all doors are open
in the chest. We want the ocean to help,
because we don't know,
we don't know how to finish.

MY MOTHER WAKES UP LATE

My mother wakes up late these days.
I help her to get up. I put on her glasses.

We walk to the bathroom. 25 steps, slowly.
I hold both her hands as if we were dancing.
She brushes her feet against the floor.
I walk backwards.

It's kind of cloudy today. She says that every morning
since her sight started to fail.

She sits on the toilet, rubs her eyes,
runs her fingers through her hair trying to remove
the remains of last night's medication.

I am about to prepare the bath. *What is that?* she says.
There is a dead moth in the bathtub.

How is she able to see it?
She cannot read anymore,
she cannot sew—she loved sewing.
Cannot watch TV—it bothers her eyes.
She still has good peripheral vision.
The doctor has told me.

The moth has left a trail behind—golden, glittery,
calligraphy written by a drunken hand.
A trail of dance and death.

It's just a moth, Mother. They come in at night, I tell her.
I clean the bathtub with toilet paper. I let the water run.

I start to remove my mother's night gown.
Five buttons on her chest.
This must be the end of summer, she says.

CLEAN-SHAVEN HEAD, SHORT BEARD

He wears a red bandana around his neck
as we go for a hike
in the Santa Barbara mountains.
Brother George is in his eighties,
doesn't carry a cane or walking stick.

He just came back from New York.
They sent me to New York because
they thought I was dying, he says.
They sent me there but after a year,
you see, I didn't die.
You have recovered, they told me.
The doctors were wrong.
And I came back to California.

We walk for more than an hour until we reach
the creek near the monastery.
Brother George picks a plant that grows by the water.
A single-leaf plant the color of young lettuce.
It's a type of watercress, he tells me.
You can eat this. Try it. He holds the stem as
if seeing the plant for the first time.

He looks like the saints on my childhood altars—
clean-shaven head, short beard,
the skin of his hands polished by age.
All of a sudden, his nose bleeds.
Brother George unties the bandana,
covers his face. *It happens to me sometimes.*
Don't worry, he says, his voice muffled.

The back of his neck is naked now,
reveals deep wrinkles—crosshatched.
His flesh is pale, kissable.
He is old and young.
I take two steps back.
He wets the bandana in the creek
and we keep walking as if nothing has happened.

CONVENIENCE STORE

I went to the convenience store,
he says. He is a family friend.
I pick him up in front of
his apartment building.
It's Thanksgiving or Passover.
I only see him twice a year.
He doesn't have a car.
He sits in the passenger seat,
complains about his knees—arthritis,
complains about not finding a job
at his age.

He smells like soap today.
I told him he couldn't come into the car
if he didn't shower.
His nails are long, ridged,
some of them split, broken,
peeling off.
Maybe some kind of mineral
deficiency, some medication's side effect.
Must be uncomfortable
to maneuver in life
with your nails getting caught everywhere—
socks, sleeves, sweaters.
I don't think he cares.

He is clean-shaven,
has missed some stubble
on the left chin—

there is always something,
it looks like an island
of dead grass.

I went to the convenience store,
he says,
*and I bought a soda
and a candy bar.
But I didn't have
enough money.
I needed 25 cents more.
The girl in the store
took out 25 cents
from her own pocket.
The next day I went back
and I put the 25 cents
in the penny jar.
I think she was happy to see me.*

How old is she? I ask.

*Probably my age,
but she looks younger,* he says.

*She opened a can of soda,
when I went back, you know,
and we passed it back and forth,* he says.
*I told her that she was pretty.
We have the same taste in music.*

I started talking about the bands I know,
because I was in a band.
I played electric guitar.
We went everywhere, in a bus.
I made a list.

You made a list. I say.

A list of all the things
I want to tell her.
I don't want to forget.
It has happened to me before,
that I forget.
I have to practice.
Can I practice with you?
Like, I think of you all the time,
and you are so kind,
and I was in a band before,
and we should go out
to a concert or something,
and I want to touch you.

He covers his face
with his hands,
like a child.

THE TRAVELER

Déjame ver la cicatriz de tu espalda.
Let me see the scar on your back, you say.

¿Qué te pasó?
What happened? you ask.
Me caí de un árbol, de pequeño.
I fell from a tree, when I was a child, I say.

You tell me about your homeland today,
faraway. You talk about horses running down the hills.
Todo tiembla con los caballos.
Everything trembles with the horses, you say.

And then you spread my arms with your arms.
And we stretch, and we touch the horses,
the solid flanks, the wet manes.

No te muevas ahora.
Don't move now, you say.

I see the carpet, its fibers,
an empty bowl of cereal, a spoon
that has been in your mouth,
like my body has been in your mouth,
like my body the spoon is clean and stained,
used, blessed and condemned, exhausted.

There is a copy of *The New Yorker*,
a poem that you once read to me.

No puedo quedarme aquí.
I cannot stay here, you say.

There are empty wine bottles on the floor
aligned against the wall. Seven bottles.
I count them from right to left.
I count them from left to right, one more time.

STREET VENDOR

Lo que le agrade, señor. Lo que le agrade.
Whatever you like, sir. Whatever you like.

The young girl is sitting on the sidewalk.
She repeats her litany with tired enthusiasm.

Vendo pulseras. Pulseras de todos los colores.
I sell bracelets. Bracelets of all colors.

It's Sunday evening and the last tourists walk back
to their hotels, warm showers and soft blankets.

She sells bracelets in the streets and train stations,
at restaurant patios before the waiters ask her to go.

She may be seven or eight, has long hair, thin wrists,
fast, precise hands, chipped nail polish.

Yo hago las pulseras, señor. Con bolsas de plástico.
I make the bracelets myself, sir. With plastic bags.

She tears the bags open with her front teeth, braids
the shreds, ties the ends. *Es fácil,* she says. *It's easy.*

She is alone, this girl. Alone like the woman I see
some mornings walking on the freeway divider.

¿Dónde encuentras las bolsas de plástico?
Where do you get the plastic bags? I ask her.

En la basura. In the trash, she says.
And "basura" sounds like amethyst, cathedral, tuberose.

A veces, pocas veces, she says, *las trae el viento.*
Sometimes, a few times, they are brought by the wind.

THEY SAY FIRE IS THE TONGUE OF GOD

Past fire extinguished inside cold volcanic rocks.
Future fire in lightning, war, and funeral pyres.
Present fire in this combustion that we are.

I drive Brother George to the monastery.
To the place where the monastery used to be.
This is his first time back there
after the fire destroyed it all.

I bring my dog Cooper with us, because he loves
Brother George, because he may help
sort out the path of grief.

It's hard to believe, Brother George says
when we arrive, standing at the edge of the road.
The tower was there, he says, pointing
at the air on a clear Sunday morning.

Workers have removed the rubble.
Brother George walks into the dark, flat, ground.
The library was there, he says. *The refectory,*
the pantry, our rooms, the main chapel.

The bell is still standing, lifted on a tall, uneven tripod.
A bell big as a horse's head, all bronze but humble.
Almost embarrassed by its survival.

Brother George rings the bell, three times,
and the sound, violent and soft, rolls down
the mountains that open like a throat.

Cooper gets agitated, starts barking to the sky,
eyes furious, leash tense. I kneel down and
cover his ears. *It's okay, it's okay,* I say.

Brother George leans his forehead against
the bell, suffocates the last breath of sound,
and all is quiet again, inescapable.

CROWN OF YOUTH

The crown of youth rattles on the floor.
We both need glasses now to read the menu.

Mine have a plain metal frame.
Yours have thick tortoiseshell rims

like the glasses of a painter or a photographer
on the back cover of an art book.

Two boring men sitting together, slightly overdressed.
We used to make fun of people like us, I remind you.

We are having dinner near the Santa Monica Pier.
You are visiting California, after all these years.

In the distance, the lights of the Ferris wheel, turning.
Wine? the waitress asks.

We look at each other. *Just water,* we say.
And, as much as we can, we pretend to be sober.

She removes the wine glasses, places them on a shelf,
next to each other, upside down.

When was the last time you were here? I ask.
More than fifteen years ago, you answer.

With careful rhythm,
you unfold the napkin over your knees.

How is your father? I ask.
Getting old, you answer. *And depressed.*

He was so handsome, I say.
Yes, he was, you say. *Still is.*

I remember your father swimming.
Sunbathing next to us, I say.

My father was young then, you say.
Younger than we are now.

The waitress comes.
We have some specials today, she says.

We don't pay much attention. We are far away
in that summer house you had in the south of England.

We are reading in the back garden, hidden
behind tall hedges. Or taking a nap.

There are apricots in a blue ceramic bowl,
a sketch book with your drawings and watercolors,

a faded-out swimsuit on the grass, your father's perhaps,
towels and blankets rolled in a basket.

There is time, and possibility,
even when the shadows stretch and it's getting cold.

I could die now, you said one day.
I didn't know how to respond.

I was used to saying what others wanted to hear.
But right then, I was not sure what you wanted.

And I didn't dare to say what I wanted.
Sudden rain with no shelter.

You place your hands on the table,
spread your fingers, smooth the tablecloth.

No wrinkles, no crumbs, just white fibers
tightly woven—a wide path between us.

The table is an expansive field of cotton. Seeds flying.
Seeds become plants, plants become seeds.

Is that a wedding band? I ask.
Yes, you say. *I got married last January.*

But you had been together for a long time, I say.
If you can call it "together," you say.

Fog comes and covers the window
like a soft shoulder sleeping against a wall.

The lights of the Ferris wheel
barely visible now. Still turning.

THE DRIVE BACK HOME

Dry pine needles inside the car.
Some of them crossed, make an "x".

There is almost nothing left now that we drive back home
after a few days on the Central Coast of California.

Almost nothing. The two of us dismantled, stripped to bone—
without the distraction of sex, without the destruction of love.

We buy a bottle of wine for your father. He is sick
in his Malibu home where he lives with his second wife.

Really sick. We almost canceled this trip.
Do we have time to stop and visit him? you ask.

It's okay, I say. We go to his house and we pretend to be happy
and he pretends to like the wine that he will never drink.

There is a picture framed on the wall; your father's last birthday.
I am in the picture, next to you. Don't recognize myself.

I move a chair to sit close to him. Its legs leave a deep indentation
on the carpet. Everything has a place, an exact distance.

He is so frail, you say, when we leave the house.
So frail, I repeat, as I reach for my seatbelt.

THE PSYCHIATRIST

I still cannot walk that street
without the cobblestones becoming
hummingbirds or egrets,
I tell my psychiatrist.

You have eroticized the landscape, he says.
We have a strange way of talking.
Lyrical. Started in our first session.
I will rebuild the architecture of your sleep, he says.
I need to return to my inner almond, I say.

The birds I see, Dr. Bradley, don't have wings, I say.
No wings, he says.
No wings, I say. *They look like feathered embryos*
with hard, open mouths.

He asks me about my adrenal glands.
I have no idea.
You should read this, he says.
He turns to get a book.
I see the back of his jacket;
silver embroidery
and a bejeweled skull, all rhinestones,
in the center.

That's a rock-star jacket, I say.
You should get one yourself, he says.
The store is right here, on Melrose.

He gives me the book.
Why Zebras Don't Get Ulcers?
That's the title. Five zebras dancing
on the cover.

What else happens when you walk on that street? he asks.
I see a girl, standing still, a child, really, I say.
Who is that girl? he asks.
I know who she is, but I don't tell him.
I don't tell him everything.

Dr. Bradley leans over the table.
He is bald on top of the head
but has long hair on the sides,
like blond, soft curtains.
He has lips injected with collagen,
upper eyelid surgery, thin scars still tender
behind his glasses.
He has long fingers, somehow arthritic,
wears a Trinity ring, by Cartier.

This child, this girl tells me to go to Madrid, I say.
I used to live in Madrid, you know,
I still have good friends there.
She tells me to go to Madrid
to visit my friends.
She knows their names, she knows where they live;
in that house behind the theater in Plaza Santa Ana.

Do you talk to this girl? Dr. Bradley asks.
She talks to me, I say. *She tells me to visit my friends,*
to stay with them for a week or so.

And then, he says.
And then, I say, *the last day,*
when they are asleep,
and I wake up early to go to the airport,
still dark outside,
and I check that I did not forget anything,
I read the note my friends left
on the bathroom mirror:
"Come back soon, we miss you."

And the girl? Dr. Bradley asks.
She tells me go to the bedroom
where my friends sleep, and kiss them one last time.
Kiss them on the neck, behind the ear,
where the soul rests like a sweet membrane,
where we all smell like birth.
Kiss them one last time
and leave a clean knife under their pillow.

She tells me to go, Dr. Bradley.
The taxi is waiting downstairs.
She tells me to hurry up.

NORTH OR SOUTH

—You are on the other side.
—No, *tú* estás en el otro lado.

A blind river without name,
un río ciego, sin nombre,
flows with outstretched arms
like a somnambulist,
como un sonámbulo.

When the river finds an edge
it becomes waterfall,
underground current,
corriente subterránea,
it becomes clouds.

La lluvia derrite los contornos.
North and South. Norte y Sur.

FOURTEEN HORSES IN
A SMALL CHAMBER

Me da miedo la tormenta, padre.
I am afraid of the storm, Father.

My father once told me
that fear waits piled up, like firewood,
outside the home of the heart.

It is your job to decide how much firewood
you want to bring inside.

Some people bring a single log,
a sliver, a shard, a splinter.

Some people carry armfuls of wood.
They stock up, they go back for seconds
as if invited to a feast.
Long-term fear, almost undetectable,
sudden fear, soft fear
that feels like company or comfort.

Tonight, wild horses rustle
in the small chamber of my heart.
Unquiet hooves. Lips twitching.
Teeth clacking like clean stones.
They want me to open the door,
to let them out into the night
and the smooth uncertainty
of wet grass and sharp breeze.

Crickets are calling. Faint music
from a faraway town is calling.

I arrange the firewood inside,
each log like an old friend that
comes to remember the past.

I count the horses' heads. Fourteen.
We are all in.
It's time to lock the door,
to taste the security of roofs and walls.

So easy to obey the hand that obeys
the fear. So easy to light the fire.

ACKNOWLEDGMENTS

Grateful acknowledgments to the editors of the following journals and anthologies in which these poems first appeared, sometimes in different versions.

Angle of Reflection: "The Actress"
Askew: "The Caretaker", "Taxi Driver"
Bridges: "North or South"
The Citron Review: "The Traveler"
The Coiled Serpent: "My Mother Wakes Up Late"
Cultural Weekly: "Old Petra"
Dark Ink: "Fourteen Horses in a Small Chamber"
The Enchanting Verses Literary Review: "Kitchen Oracle"
Incandescent Mind: "Convenience Store"
LARB: "The Actor"
Levure Littéraire: "Woman Without a Nose", "The Neighbor"
        (published as "At His House")
Monster Verse: "Sireno (Merboy)"
The New Guard: "The Philosopher"
Oberon: "The Drive Back Home"
Pinyon: "Figs"
Poeming Pigeons: "Decoding Sparrows"
River's Voice: "The Card Player"
Spillway: "They Say Fire is the Tongue of God"
Tupelo Quarterly: "Plums"
Wide Awake: "Red Swimsuits", "Baldomera"
Women in Metaphor: "Portrait and Still Life with Art"
Zócalo Public Square: "Nun Eating a Small Apple", "On Being Jewish, Perhaps"

Deep gratitude to the following poets for their help editing these poems. This book would not have been possible without you: Javier Albo, Tony Barnstone, Marjorie Becker, Jeanette Clough, Mariana Dietl, Theresa Freije, Dina Hardy, Jennifer Holmes, Paul Lieber, Sarah Maclay, Holaday Mason, Jim Natal, Jan Wesley and Brenda Yates.

MARIANO ZARO is the author of four bilingual books of poetry, most recently *Tres letras/Three Letters* (Walrus, Barcelona). His poems have been published in the anthologies *Monster Verse* (Penguin Random House), *Wide Awake* (Beyond Baroque), *The Coiled Serpent* (Tía Chucha Press), *Angle of Reflection* (Arctos Press) and in several magazines in Spain, Mexico and the United States.

His translations include *Poemas de las Misiones de California* by Philomene Long, *Buda en llamas* by Tony Barnstone and, in collaboration with Estíbaliz Espinosa and Amaia Gabantxo, *Cómo escribir una canción de amor* by Sholeh Wolpé.

Zaro's short stories have appeared in *Portland Review, Pinyon, Baltimore Review, Louisville Review* and *Magnapoets*. He is the winner of the 2004 Roanoke Review Short Fiction Prize and the 2018 Martha's Vineyard Institute of Creative Writing Short Fiction Prize.

Since 2010, he has been hosting a series of video-interviews with prominent American poets as part of the literary project Poetry.LA.

Mariano Zaro earned a Ph.D. in Linguistics from the University of Granada (Spain) and a Master's in Literature from the University of Zaragoza (Spain). He is a professor of Spanish at Rio Hondo Community College (Whittier, California).

WHAT BOOKS PRESS

LOS ANGELES

CPSIA information can be obtained
at www.ICGtesting.com
Printed in the USA
LVHW092304200120
644178LV00007B/584